ABORTION!

IS IT PRO-LIFE OR PRO-CHOICE?

Diana Prager

Contents

INTRODUCTION

Fetus removal regulations differ generally among nations and domains, and have changed over the long run. Such regulations range from fetus removal being openly accessible on demand, to guideline or limitations of different sorts, to altogether denial in all conditions. Numerous nations and domains that permit fetus removal have gestational cutoff points for the methodology relying upon the explanation; with the larger part being as long as 12 weeks for early termination on demand, as long as 24 weeks for assault, interbreeding, or financial reasons, and something else for fetal weakness or endanger to the lady's wellbeing or life. Starting around 2022, nations that legitimately permit early termination on demand or for financial reasons include around 60% of the total populace.

There are no worldwide or global arrangements that manage early termination yet common liberties regulation and Global criminal regulation touch on the issues. Early termination keeps on being a dubious subject in numerous social orders on strict, moral, moral, viable, and political grounds. However it has been restricted and generally restricted by regulation in numerous locales, early terminations keep on being normal in numerous areas, even where they are unlawful. As per a recent report led by the Guttmacher Establishment and the World Wellbeing Association (WHO), fetus removal rates are comparable in nations where the methodology is lawful and in nations where it isn't, because of inaccessibility of current contraceptives in regions where early termination is unlawful. Additionally as per the review, the quantity of early terminations overall is declining because of expanded admittance to contraception.

HISTORY

Fetus removal has existed since old times, with regular abortifacients being found among a wide assortment of ancestral individuals and in most composed sources. The earliest known records of fetus removal methods and general regenerative guideline date as far back as 2700 BC in China, and 1550 BC in Egypt. Early texts contain little notice of fetus removal or fetus removal regulation. At the point when it shows up, it is involved in worries about male property privileges, conservation of social request, and the obligation to deliver fit residents for the state or local area. The cruelest punishments were for the most part held for a lady early termination against her better half's desires, and for slaves who delivered fetus removal in a lady of high status. Strict texts frequently contained extreme judgments of early termination, suggesting repentance yet only sometimes upholding mainstream discipline. As an issue of precedent-based regulation in Britain and the US, early termination was unlawful any time in the wake of reviving — when the developments of the baby could initially be felt by the lady. Under the conceived alive rule, the baby was not viewed as a "sensible being" in rerum natura; and early termination was not treated as murder in English regulation.

In the twentieth hundred years, numerous Western nations started to systematize fetus removal regulations or put further limitations on the training. Hostile to early termination developments, likewise alluded to as "favorable to life" developments, were driven by a blend of gatherings went against to fetus removal on moral grounds, and by clinical experts who were worried about the peril introduced by the methodology and the customary contribution of non-clinical staff in performing fetus removals. In any case, obviously unlawful fetus removals kept on occurring in huge numbers even where early terminations were thoroughly limited. It was challenging to get adequate proof to indict the ladies and early termination specialists, and judges and juries were frequently hesitant to convict. For instance, Henry Morgentaler, a Canadian supportive of decision advocate, was never indicted by a jury. He was vindicated by a jury in the 1973 legal dispute, yet the quittance was toppled by five adjudicators on the Quebec Court of Allure in 1974. He went to jail, pursued, and was again absolved. Altogether, he served 10 months, experiencing a coronary failure while in isolation. Many were additionally shocked at the intrusion of security and the clinical issues coming about because of early terminations occurring unlawfully in medicinally perilous conditions. Political developments before long mixed around the authorization of fetus removal and advancement of existing regulations.

By the principal half of the twentieth 100 years, numerous nations had started to change early termination regulations, basically when performed to safeguard the lady's life and at times on the lady's solicitation. Under Vladimir Lenin, the Soviet Association turned into the principal present day state in sanctioning early terminations on demand — the law was first presented in the Russian SFSR in 1920, in the Ukrainian SSR in July 1921, and afterward in the entire country. The Marxists saw fetus removal as a social underhanded made by the entrepreneur framework, which passed on ladies without the monetary means to bring up youngsters, driving them to perform early terminations. The Soviet state at first safeguarded the tsarist restriction on fetus removal, which regarded the training as planned murder. Nonetheless, early termination had been rehearsed by Russian individuals for quite a long time and its frequency soar further because of the Russian Nationwide conflict, which had left the nation monetarily crushed and made it very hard for some individuals to have kids. The Soviet state perceived that restricting early termination wouldn't stop the training since ladies would keep utilizing the administrations of private abortionists. In country regions, these were in many cases elderly people ladies who had no clinical preparation, which made their administrations extremely perilous to ladies' wellbeing. In November 1920 the Soviet system legitimized fetus removal in state emergency clinics. The state considered fetus removal as a transitory means to an end, which would vanish later on socialist society, which would have the option to accommodate every one of the youngsters conceived.] In 1936, Joseph Stalin put forbiddances on early terminations, which confined them to medicinally suggested cases just, to increment populace development after the gigantic death toll in The Second Great War and the Russian

Nationwide conflict. During the 1930s, a few nations (Poland, Turkey, Denmark, Sweden, Iceland, and Mexico) sanctioned early termination in a few unique cases (pregnancy from assault, danger to mother's wellbeing, fetal contortion). In Japan, early termination was sanctioned in 1948 by the Eugenic Security Regulation, corrected in May 1949 to permit fetus removals for financial reasons. Fetus removal was legitimized in 1952 in Yugoslavia (on a restricted premise, and again in 1955 in the Soviet Association on demand. A few Soviet partners (Poland, Hungary, Bulgaria, Czechoslovakia, Romania sanctioned early termination in the last part of the 1950s under tension from the Soviets.

In the Unified Realm, the Early termination Demonstration of 1967 explained and recommended fetus removals as lawful as long as (after 28 weeks decreased to 24 weeks). Different nations before long followed, including Canada (1969), the US (1973 in many states, according to Roe v. Swim — the U.S. High Court choice which legitimized fetus removal from one side of the country to the other), Tunisia and Denmark (1973), Austria (1974), France and Sweden (1975), New Zealand (1977), Italy (1978), the Netherlands (1984), and Belgium (1990). Notwithstanding, these nations fluctuate enormously in the conditions under which early termination was to be allowed. In 1975, the West German High Court struck down a regulation sanctioning fetus removal, holding that they go against the constitution's common freedoms ensures. In 1976, a regulation was embraced which empowered fetus removals as long as 12 weeks. After Germany's reunification, in spite of the legitimate status of early termination in previous East Germany, a trade off was arrived at which considered most fetus removals as long as 12 weeks legitimate, yet this regulation was struck somewhere near the Government Sacred Court and corrected to just eliminate the discipline in such cases, with no assertion to lawfulness. In purviews represented under sharia regulation, fetus removal after the 120th day from origination (19 weeks from LMP) is unlawful, particularly for the people who follow the suggestions of the Hanafi lawful school, while most law specialists of the Maliki legitimate school "accept that ensoulment happens right now of origination, and they will generally deny early termination anytime [similar to the Roman Catholic Church]. Different schools stand firm on transitional situations. The punishment endorsed for an unlawful early termination differs as indicated by specific conditions included. As indicated by sharia, it ought to be restricted to a fine that is paid to the dad or main successors to the baby."

ABORTION FACTS

An early termination is an operation that closes a pregnancy. It is an essential medical care need for a great many ladies, young ladies and other people who can become pregnant. Around the world, an expected 1 out of 4 pregnancies end in an early termination each year.25 million perilous fetus removals occur every year.

In any case, while the requirement for fetus removal is normal, admittance to protected and lawful early termination administrations is a long way from ensured for the people who might require fetus removal administrations.

ABORTION

As a matter of fact, admittance to fetus removal is one of the most controversial points worldwide, and the discussion is blurred by falsehood about the genuine implications of limiting admittance to this essential medical care administration.

Fundamental Realities ABOUTABORTION:

Individuals have early terminations constantly, paying little mind to what the law says

Finishing a pregnancy is a typical choice that great many individuals make - consistently a fourth of pregnancies end in early termination.

Furthermore, whether or not early termination is lawful or not, individuals actually require and consistently access fetus removal administrations. As per the Guttmacher Foundation, a US-based regenerative wellbeing non-benefit, the fetus removal rate is 37 for each 1,000 individuals in nations that preclude early termination through and through or permit it just in occasions to save a lady's life, and 34 for every 1,000 individuals in nations that comprehensively consider early termination, a distinction that isn't genuinely critical.

At the point when embraced by a prepared medical care supplier in clean circumstances, early terminations are perhaps of the most secure operation accessible, more secure even than labor.

However, when legislatures confine admittance to early terminations, individuals are constrained to depend on undercover, dangerous fetus removals, especially the people who can't bear to travel or look for private consideration. Which carries us to the following point?

Condemning early termination doesn't stop fetus removals; it simply makes early termination less protected

Keeping ladies and young ladies from getting to a fetus removal doesn't mean they quit requiring one. That is the reason endeavors to boycott or limit fetus removals never really diminish the quantity of early terminations, it just powers individuals to search out dangerous early terminations.

Dangerous fetus removals are characterized by the World Wellbeing Association (WHO) as "a method for ending an accidental pregnancy completed either by people without the essential abilities or in a climate that doesn't adjust to negligible clinical norms, or both."

They gauge those 25 million risky fetus removals happen every year, by far most of them in non-industrial nations.

Rather than a lawful fetus removal that is completed by a prepared clinical supplier, dangerous early terminations can have deadly results. To such an extent that dangerous early terminations are the third driving reason for maternal passing's overall and lead to an extra 5,000,000 generally preventable inabilities, as per the WHO.

A demonstrator paints a legend in the city popular of ladies' admittance to protected, free and lawful early termination, during a meeting outside the Public Congress in Buenos Aires, on April 10, 2018.

Pretty much every passing and injury from risky fetus removal is preventable

Passing's and wounds from dangerous early terminations are preventable. However such passings are normal in nations where admittance to safe fetus removal is restricted or precluded, as most of ladies and young ladies who need an early termination due to an undesirable pregnancy can't lawfully get to one.

In nations with such limitations, the law regularly considers what are known as restricted exemptions for the regulation condemning fetus removal. These exemptions may be when pregnancy results from assault or inbreeding, in instances of extreme and lethal fetal hindrance, or when there is endanger to the life or strength of the pregnant individual. Just a little level of fetus removals are because of these reasons, meaning most of ladies and young ladies living under these regulations may be compelled to look for dangerous early terminations and endangered their wellbeing and lives.

The people who are now underestimated are excessively impacted by such regulations as they have no means to look for protected and lawful administrations in another nation or access private consideration. They remember ladies and young ladies for low pay, exiles and travelers, teenagers, lesbian, sexually unbiased cisgender ladies and young ladies, transsexual or orientation non-adjusting people, minority or Native ladies.

The WHO has noticed that one of the most vital moves toward keeping away from maternal passing's and wounds is for states to guarantee that individuals approach sex instruction, can utilize successful contraception, have protected and legitimate early termination, and are given convenient consideration for complexities.

Proof shows that early termination rates are higher in nations where there is restricted admittance to contraception. Early termination rates are lower where individuals, including teenagers have data about and can get to current preventative techniques and where far reaching sexuality instruction is accessible and there is admittance to protected and lawful fetus removal on wide grounds.

ABORTION

Numerous nations are beginning to change their regulations to take into account more noteworthy admittance to fetus removal

Throughout recent years, in excess of 50 nations have changed their regulations to consider more noteworthy admittance to early termination, now and again perceiving the essential job that admittance to safe fetus removal plays in safeguarding ladies' lives and wellbeing. Ireland joined that rundown on 25 May 2018 when, in a hotly anticipated mandate, its kin casted a ballot predominantly to cancel the close complete established restriction on fetus removal.

In spite of the pattern towards transforming regulations to forestall passing's and wounds, a few nations, including Nicaragua and El Salvador, keep up with draconian unfair regulations that actually boycott fetus removal in practically all conditions. As a matter of fact, as per the WHO, across the globe 40% of ladies of childbearing age live in nations with exceptionally prohibitive fetus removal regulations, or where early termination is legitimate, is neither accessible nor open. In these states, early termination is prohibited or just allowed in exceptionally limited conditions, or on the other hand in the event that lawful, isn't open because of numerous boundaries to access by and by.

Indeed, even in states with more extensive admittance to legitimate early termination, pregnant people can in any case confront various limitations on and boundaries to admittance to administrations like expense, one-sided guiding, and obligatory holding up periods. The WHO has given specialized direction for states on the need to distinguish and eliminate such boundaries.

Condemning or limiting early termination keeps specialists from giving essential consideration

Criminalization and prohibitive regulations on early termination keep medical services suppliers from going about their business appropriately and from giving the best consideration choices to their patients, in accordance with great clinical practice and their expert moral obligations.

Criminalization of early termination results in a "chilling impact", by which clinical experts may not figure out the limits of the law or may apply the limitations in a smaller manner than expected by the law. This might be a direct result of various reasons, including individual convictions, shame about fetus removal, negative generalizations about ladies and young ladies, or the feeling of dread toward criminal risk.

It likewise stops ladies and young ladies from looking for post-fetus removal care for entanglements because of perilous early termination or other pregnancy related difficulties.

It's not simply cisgender ladies and young ladies who need early terminations

It isn't just cisgender ladies and young ladies (ladies and young ladies who were doled out female upon entering the world) who might require admittance to fetus removal administrations, yet additionally intersex individuals, transsexual men and young men, and individuals with other orientation personalities who have the conceptive ability to become pregnant.

One of the preeminent obstructions to early termination access for these people and gatherings is absence of admittance to medical care. Furthermore, for the people who really do approach medical care, they might confront shame and one-sided sees in the arrangement of medical services, as well as assumptions that they needn't bother with admittance to contraception and early termination related data and administrations. In certain unique circumstances, 28% transsexual and orientation non-adjusting people report confronting badgering in clinical settings, and 19% report being rejected clinical consideration by and large because of their transsexual status, with considerably bigger numbers among networks of variety. This is because of many entwining elements of destitution and race and related interconnected segregation.

Sexual and conceptive freedoms advocates and LGBTI privileges activists are lobbying for bringing issues to light on this and making early termination administrations accessible available and comprehensive for every individual who needs it without separation on any grounds.

Condemning fetus removal is a type of separation, which further fills disgrace

Right off the bat, the forswearing of clinical benefits, includes conceptive wellbeing administrations that main certain people need is a type of segregation.

The panel for the Unified Countries Show on the Disposal of All Types of Oppression Ladies (CEDAW, or the Arrangement for the Privileges of Ladies), has reliably expressed that prohibitive fetus removal regulations comprise victimization ladies. This applies to all ladies and individuals who can become pregnant, as the CEDAW Board has affirmed that CEDAW's securities, and states' connected commitments, apply to all ladies and subsequently incorporate victimization ladies who are lesbians, sexually open, and additionally transsexual, especially given the particular types of gendered separation they face.

Besides, shame around early termination and orientation generalizing is firmly connected to the criminalization of fetus removal and other prohibitive fetus removal regulations and arrangements.

The simple discernment that fetus removal is unlawful or corrupt prompts the criticism of ladies and young ladies by medical care staff, relatives, and the legal executive, among others. Subsequently, ladies and young ladies looking for early termination risk segregation and provocation. A few ladies have detailed being manhandled and disgraced by medical care suppliers while looking for early termination administrations or post-fetus removal care.

Admittance to safe fetus removal involves basic freedom

Admittance to safe fetus removal administrations is a basic freedom. Under global common liberties regulation, everybody has a privilege to life, a right to wellbeing, and an option to be liberated from viciousness, separation, and torment or brutal, barbaric and corrupting treatment.

Basic freedoms regulation obviously illuminates that choices about your body are yours alone - this is known as substantial independence.

Compelling somebody to carry on an undesirable pregnancy, or driving them to search out a perilous early termination, is an infringement of their basic freedoms, including the privileges to security and substantial independence.

Much of the time, the people who must choose the option to fall back on hazardous fetus removals likewise risk arraignment and discipline, including detainment, and can confront brutal, barbaric and debasing treatment and separation in, and rejection from, fundamental post-early termination medical services.

Admittance to early termination is consequently essentially connected to safeguarding and maintaining the common liberties of ladies, young ladies and other people who can become pregnant, and in this way for accomplishing social and orientation equity.

Reprieve Global accepts that everybody ought to be allowed to practice their substantial independence and arrive at their own conclusions about their conceptive lives including when and assuming they have kids. It is fundamental that regulations connecting with early termination regard secure and satisfy the common liberties of pregnant people and not drive them to search out dangerous fetus removals.

PROS OF ABORTION

There are a couple of disputes that one forward on early end. In particular, any birth of a young person should happen at whatever point the watchmen need and not by some occurrence. This way it would go very far in assisting the world with having an environment where all youths that are brought into the world in this world have an environment positive for genuine development.

There is no prerequisite for expanding the world with various children who can't move toward fundamental necessities like good clothing, food, shelter, and preparing. It should moreover be seen that when an individual decides to finish an early end it isn't out of her revultion for youngsters yet since she feels that it wouldn't be a canny decision to go on with the pregnancy for all intents and purposes at this point not yet the ideal chance to have a kid.

By virtue of attack or inbreeding, keeping a pregnancy is exceptionally harming to the individual attacked as no one would wish to keep a youngster that is an outcome of this, and the most fitting solution for this issue is stopped the unborn young person.

For the occasion of attack, the significant effects of the occasion are excessively harming and cut out an amazing open door to patch, and some attack losses recover in no way, shape or form. Adding a young person to the attack setback looks like adding more salt to a physical issue and would be a consistent update that is presumably going to add more significant injury to the individual being referred to.

Numerous examinations on the significant quality or obscenities of hatchling evacuation have found that a part of those against the moral nature of early end will by and large agree that alright to stop a pregnancy is an outcome of attack.

For instance, the swallow review did in Canada considered to be only 13% of the respondents were against the preparation absolutely while inquisitively a dumbfounding 65% were of the view that it is alright to stop an unfortunate pregnancy in unambiguous conditions like expecting that it is a result of attack.

There has moreover been an interminable conversation on the particular time that an undeveloped organism protects life and transforms into a person with honors and ability to have feelings. Sather further battles that before the 24th-28th week, the child has not yet gotten human features and it doesn't amount to kill expecting you play out an early end before this time.

Good for lifers drove by the Catholic Church request that life begins at start and any person who is viewed as to blame for having played out an early end could be restricted from the gathering because of doing kill. That isn't every one of the couple of assessments when life stars by virtue of an unborn youth have achieved conflicting dates.

ABORTION

The approaching impasse regarding, when an individual can and can't have an embryo evacuation, have given it plausible for anyone to lead an early end. It isn't clear concerning when life begins, and as while a woman feels that she can't have a kid, she has the potential chance to do it since it isn't yet clear when the presence of a singular beginnings.

Sometimes intricacies can happen to a pregnancy that could put the presence of the mother or unborn young person at serious gamble and, surprisingly, once in a while all of them. For this present circumstance, early end ought to be permitted to save the genuine sufficiency of the mother but a piece of those maintaining for baby evacuation have regularly fought that the profound prosperity of the mother ought to be consolidated while examining prosperity

At this point, the presence of the mother is given previously thought as the hatchling can't manage without the mother, and notwithstanding, the chances are the mother can continually get various youths if she wants, but it is totally unthinkable that a child can make due with its let be getting various gatekeepers which is incredible.

CONS OF ABORTION

A couple of bothers of early end are battled out by strong of lifers. Most of the books in regards to the matter are by and large on the burdens of early end when diverged from the advantages. According to Genuine hatchling evacuation is only a fleeting and counter-intuitive decision that makes women feel that they have gotten an assistance to an unfortunate young person against chances of incredibly strong loss of infertility.

She further fights that notwithstanding the way that

disposing of a bothersome pregnancy may somehow recommendation help to the woman the possibility becoming unbeneficial especially expecting an ill-suited individual played out the movement is incredibly basic and when you lose your wealth there is zero chance that you will recover it.

Regardless, when performed by a confirmed clinical expert potentially traps could arise like in a couple of tasks and if this happens; you could lose your productivity. Indeed, interviews drove on women who had burdens while playing out an early end revealed that a bigger piece of them had lost the ability to consider or hard an unexpected labor .

The assistance that one feels following getting an early end is for the most part short lived, and it kicks the can after some time inciting an incredibly strong vibe of culpability and inconvenience. Truly, in a huge part of the times, this freeing sensation is just a cognizant undertaking by the mind study of a person to eradicate the sensation of culpability and shame that hauls in rapidly one gets a baby expulsion.

Holman further adds that but most of the guideline and procedures concerning early end license the preparation by virtue of understudies that you once killed piece of you isn't presumably going to vanish and will torture you always and forever.

A lot of great for lifers would compare baby evacuation to murder, and it is thusly morally misguided and should be disallowed. Genovese portrays murder as a deliberate show of eliminating the presence of a person .Fro this he further adds that since the hatchling of an individual has life, then, eliminating it will amount to killing it, which is identical to kill.

Clearly from this reason disputes will without a doubt arise in regards to when the presence of an individual truly begins. To all Christians drove by the Catholic Church, it is absolutely unsatisfactory to allow a person to eliminate another person's life for whichever reason and at anything that stage in life as it is still homicide. The late Pope John Paul is on record as having reprimanded the preparation and regardless, communicating that it would think twice about a valuable open door and balance of humankind as it progresses a culture of enduring passing as something run of the mill.

Getting a baby expulsion isn't the primary plan there of psyche of unwanted pregnancy as the youngster could moreover be put to gathering. It is surveyed that in evidently hitched couples in the US alone, between 10% - 15% of them don't can have young people.

This figure is high so much that a steadily expanding number of Americans are going to various countries abroad to get posterity of their own and as Grunlan further adds; this figure has been growing in the new years as extra mothers go to early end as a way to deal with controlling birth.

In addition, as Zastrow and Kirst add, in this age where there are such endless open prophylactic procedures; there should be very irrelevant unfortunate pregnancies that warrant the need to stop a youngster who has recently been envisioned.

ABORTION

PROS	CONS
Early termination is a protected operation that safeguards lives.	Life starts at origination, making fetus removal murder.
Early termination boycotts imperils medical services for those not looking for abortions.	Legal fetus removal advances a culture in which life is expendable.
Early termination boycotts deny substantially independence, making far reaching repercussion .	Increased admittance to conception prevention, health care coverage, and sexual instruction would make fetus removal

	pointless.

ABORTION

ABORTION

RELATIONSHIP BETWEEN RELIGION AND ABORTION

'Thou shalt not kill." (Exodus 20:13)

In the Ten Commandments , Prpverbs says "hands that shed honest blood" are one of the seven things God abhors.

God let Noah know that the taking of honest human existence was a serious offense in Genesis 9:6.

The fundamental worry in the early termination contention is whether it is ethically and morally right or wrong. Morals and profound quality are essentially examined

The central concern is the way to realize what is correct and what's going on. As contended by Aristotle in piece of the course, to become moral he ought to initially reason well and have great person, and add up to satisfaction must be accomplished in the event that individuals are honorable.

The fetus removal banter focuses on morals in that while the people who are for early termination contends that it offers an answer for heaps of issues that could be achieved by having undesirable youngsters, those against it contend that this help is short-term.

Unit three of the course is mostly on the best way to carry on with a decent life as Christians. In this fundamental part, the unit bargains on adequate Christian ideals and values. One such goodness is having unrestricted love towards others. On early termination, it is contended that when one plays out a fetus removal naturally, she doesn't have love for that kid no matter what the circumstances.

Besides, all Christians ought to safeguard human existence and have regard for Divine beings manifestations, and inability to do a transgression is as well. Individuals are likewise expected to consider basically their activities and be considered responsible to these activities, and, as examined in the unit, they ought to abstain from looking for convenient solution answers for issues confronting them.

The Catholic Church has been the most vocal in denouncing fetus removal for quite a while, and the way things are, there is no way that this strong stand will be returned. In the book Catholic profound quality and human sexuality, the writer contends that following treatment, the subsequent zygote has human elements and ought to be regarded as a person. Eliminating it from the uterus adds up to kill.

Moreover, in the event that you reject human existence anytime, it resembles dismissing God as people are made in the picture of God. Tolerating early termination has been contended by the congregation as tolerating a culture of death and living without Jesus Christ as it adds up to killing a blameless animal of God who has not yet played out any wrongdoing.

Indeed, even in instances of assault or inbreeding, the congregation doesn't allow early termination. For this situation, a lady might look for treatment following the occurrence however not early termination weeks after the episode, and regardless of whether the pregnancy is a danger to human existence, there ought to be an endeavor to save the two carries on with living souls are sacrosanct and equivalent before God a none is exceptional to the next.

SPECIAL CASES IN FETUS REMOVAL REGULATIONS

Special cases in fetus removal regulations happen either in nations where early termination is when in doubt unlawful or in nations that have early termination on demand with gestational cutoff points. For instance, in the event that a nation permits fetus removal on demand until 12 weeks, it might make exemptions for this overall growth limit for later early terminations in unambiguous conditions.

There are a couple of exemptions normally tracked down in early termination regulations. Legitimate spaces which don't have fetus removal on request will frequently permit it when the wellbeing of the mother is in question. "Wellbeing of the mother" may mean something else in various regions: for instance, proceeding December 2018, the Republic of Ireland permitted early termination just to save the mother's life, while fetus removal rivals in the US contend wellbeing exemptions are utilized so comprehensively as to deliver a boycott basically negligible.

Regulations permitting fetus removal in instances of assault or inbreeding frequently contrast. For instance, before Roe v. Swim, thirteen U.S. states permitted fetus removal on account of one or the other assault or inbreeding, however just Mississippi allowed early termination of pregnancies because of assault, and no state allowed it for just interbreeding.

Numerous nations permit early termination just through the first or second trimester, and some might permit fetus removal in instances of fetal imperfections, e.g., Down condition, or where the pregnancy is the consequence of a sexual wrongdoing.

CONCLUSION

As a general rule, it very well may be presumed that the drive on the determinants and results of prompted fetus removal has shown a few significant examples. For instance, actuated early termination isn't confined to young people however happens additionally inside union with limit family size. Incited fetus removal is pervasive both where family arranging administrations are accessible and preventative predominance is high as well as where family arranging isn't normal, yet for various reasons. In the previous, inspiration to restrict family size is high and ladies would utilize any choice assuming that contraception fizzles or an undesirable pregnancy happens. In the last option case, prompted fetus removal shapes part of a blend of early fruitfulness guideline choices, the vast majority of which are customary and of little viability however including some utilization or ill-advised utilization of present day techniques. Not many fetus removal searchers, and among them considerably less teenagers, were utilizing a cutting edge preventative at the time the pregnancy began. High utilization of customary techniques in certain nations prompts early termination as ladies/couples neglect to adhere to appropriate directions with respect to the protected period. Hazardous surreptitious early terminations are bound to be looked for by less fortunate ladies and by teenagers. The discoveries of this examination are progressively being utilized to scrutinize the legitimate status of early termination in nations where the law is prohibitive, or to reinforce family arranging endeavors to lessen fetus removal frequency.

Fetus removal has been a disputable term since the old times. In a real sense, the term is utilized to allude to the demonstration of finishing a pregnancy up, by either removing an undeveloped organism or the baby before development. Unintentional early termination is known as premature delivery; be that as it may, planned type of fetus removal is what we call initiated early termination. For some situation it is alluded to as the late end of pregnancy; the expulsion of the embryo is done when it can possibly make due in the external climate. In created nations the training has been permitted under specific circumstances, and it is finished utilizing current methods, which are protected and deal with the future wellbeing, physical, organic, and mental necessities of the person. Utilization of current careful strategies and drug followed up by family arranging techniques, similar to the pill, to keep up with the existence of the lady in a typical manner. This solid methodology doesn't open the lady to long haul results of early termination, which are both mental and physical. Conversely, north of 47000 individuals capitulate to death in view of fetus removal and more than 5 million get confined to bed every year due to actuated early termination. In the new past, the early termination rates quickly expanded to up to 56 million cases in 2002. Be that as it may, there was a surprising diminishing of the cases from 2003 to 2008 which was credited to the gigantic missions on family arranging and the utilization of condoms.

Moral, State and strict perspectives on early termination shift from one spot to another. In a few locales, the demonstration is permitted in specific circumstances like assault, natural issues, in the event that the lady's life in jeopardized, or interbreeding. Notwithstanding, early termination has stayed a far from being obviously true issue ethically, morally and lawfully. However the World Wellbeing Association has suggested more secure and legitimate techniques for early termination and a few States even legitimized it.

In a recap, it is clear that early termination presents many dangers to the lady that jeopardizes her life, yet additionally the existence of the child in resulting pregnancies. The dangers range from physical, mental to organic. Nonetheless, it is exceptionally sad that various early termination cases, effects and, surprisingly, the people who make a section in the move wrongfully go unreported. There are likewise numerous legends going circuitous the training. Nonetheless, even according to the strict perspective early termination can't be legitimate.

www.ingramcontent.com/pod-product-compliance
Lightning Source LLC
LaVergne TN
LVHW050332160826
845677LV00014B/3599